Alistair Bryce-Clegg

CONTINUOUS PROVISION

IN THE EARLY YEARS

How to plan provision to make a positive impact on children's learning

Published 2013 by Featherstone Education
Bloomsbury Publishing plc
50 Bedford Square, London WC1B 3DP
www.bloomsbury.com

Bloomsbury is a registered trademark of Bloomsbury Publishing Plc

ISBN 978-1-4081-7582-8
Text © Alistair Bryce-Clegg 2013
Design © Lynda Murray
Photographs © Shutterstock

Printed and bound in Great Britain by Ashford Colour Press Ltd

10   9   8   7   6

This book is produced using paper that is made from wood grown in
managed, sustainable forests. It is natural, renewable and recyclable.
The logging and manufacturing processes conform to the environmental
regulations of the country of origin.

To see our full range of titles visit www.bloomsbury.com

Acknowledgements
Photographs with kind permission of London Early Years Foundation/Emli Bendixen,
and Acorn Childcare Ltd.

Special thanks to:
Fee Bryce-Clegg
St Thomas Mores RC Primary School
Saint Augustines RC Primary School
The Friars Primary School
Joseph Cash Primary School
Chester Blue Coat Primary School
The Arches Primary School

Penguin Pre-School
Holton Lodge Primary School
Middlefield Primary School
Woodhouse Community Primary
Mabel Bryce
Luca Bryce

Contents

What is continuous provision?

As early years Foundation Stage (EYFS) practitioners a great many of us are about to get bashed over the head with a big stick called 'school readiness'! I have already encountered numerous settings (schools in particular) where this phrase is being interpreted as a green light to go back to formality and get the tables back out of the store cupboard.

There is often a large gap between the quality practice that is taking place in EYFS and the knowledge of the person who is making judgments about impact and attainment and that is because often, they are not sure what it is they are looking at. A more formal approach to teaching makes it easier to make those judgments.

In the past, headteachers have said to me that they can see how the children are learning when they are with an adult, but when they are playing in the environment they find it had to see evidence of attainment taking place. When it comes to how a lot of us use our continuous provision, then I think they have a valid point.

Understanding continuous provision

Mainly, I think continuous provision is greatly misunderstood. Once we get the definition of what continuous provision should be right, then quality and attainment will follow.

Continuous provision is not just the resources that you have out all of the time. The purpose of continuous provision is:

 To continue the provision for learning in the absence of an adult.

In any area where you organise a range of resources and a group of children there will be potential to develop those children's skills in personal interaction and exploration, but unless those resources have been carefully selected to meet the development needs of those specific children, then the learning potential is limited and greatly left to chance.

If you think about what you know about children, when they get the chance to 'choose' what to do they tend to pick things that they like and can do. This is just basic human nature. I have yet to meet an EYFS child who will make the conscious decision to walk into an area of continuous provision and actively challenge themselves. How many times have you commented that the same boys are in the construction/building area doing the same sorts of models and that a group of girls are back at the writing table drawing and colouring?

What we also do in early years settings is mistake compliance with engagement and attainment. You will get lots of children who are very happy to stay in an area of the provision for sustained periods of time. They will comply to the agreed behaviour code and will often be prolific in their output. But if we look at what they have produced and then ask ourselves if it shows challenge and learning, or just low level consolidation of a skill that they already had, then we are far more likely to see that it is the latter.

Where this is the case, we are not continuing the provision for learning we are 'holding' children until an adult gets to them and boosts their attainment with their input. If you think about how long some of our children spend in this level of provision without adult input then this has huge implications for potential lack of attainment.

So, if your continuous provision is just a selection of resources linked to a general area of development, then when a child is playing there their opportunities for learning are limited. Because as well as providing opportunities for exploration and discovery, your continuous provision has to be linked to your assessment of your current cohort. If it is going to be available all of the time and children are going to access it with limited adult input, it has to be structured around their developmental needs and dressed to reflect their interests.

Chapter 1

Setting up continuous provision

Consider these questions about your basic continuous provision:

- Could you stand in front of each and every area of continuous provision in your setting and tell me how what is in that area is directly linked to your observation and assessment of your children?

- Can you show me the assessment and link it to specific resources?

- Does the size of your area of continuous provision reflect the needs of your cohort? If you have children who need to develop language and talk skills, have you significantly increased the size of those areas?

- Have you levelled your continuous provision, linked to assessment so that you can show which resources have been placed in there linked to the development of high, middle and low achievers in that area?

- If we were standing in front of your mark making area could you show me how you had set that space up to reflect the mark making development of your current cohort?

- Have you got resources in place that are specifically aimed at each stage of their mark making development?

Most importantly, consider if you have 'dressed' specific resources to appeal to the group of children that you are targeting. So, if you have a group of girls with developed fine motor skills who are interested in playing princesses and a group of boys who are more gross motor skilled and interested in adventure play, you could create two boxes of resources one that contains lots of things that challenge and develop fine motor skills and another that challenges and develops more gross motor. However, if you just put these two boxes in your mark making area then the target group of children might, perhaps, maybe come in and pick up the correct resource, or maybe not!

So, you need to 'dress' the fine motor resources and the box in a princess theme and the gross motor resources and box in an adventure theme. One of the gross motor target boys is then more likely to come into the mark making area in the first place because of the resources provided. Once he's in there he is more likely to put his hands in the adventure box than the princess one and he is therefore significantly more likely to be accessing a resource that has been specifically chosen to help his development.

Of course, you cannot guarantee that this will happen every time, but what you can do is say with confidence that you have maximised the potential for attainment in continuous provision and minimised the risk of failure. Now when anyone asks you if you can quantify attainment outside of focused teaching, the job just got a whole lot easier and as a practitioner, you can be secure in the knowledge that your continuous provision is really continuing the provision for learning and isn't just a collection of nice resources.

There is so much that you can do to ensure that your environment has a huge role to play in impacting on attainment that this short example only begins to scrape the surface but hopefully it has got you thinking!

Outdoor provision

I appreciate that for many early years providers the outdoor provision is still the part of the curriculum delivery that presents a great deal of challenge. Maybe not so much in just getting the children out there, but in how to provide quality learning and not just 'playtime'.

What we should all be aiming for is equality between indoors and out in terms of planning, resourcing and use. We need to think of our indoor and outdoor together as one big space and not two separate ones. Some children prefer to learn outdoors and the outdoor environment can offer so many unique opportunities that indoors just cannot. Although there are many links between indoor and outdoor play, outdoor play offers additional opportunities to develop and extend specific skills.

When you are thinking about your outdoor provision, first look to your assessment and see which areas of skill development are priorities for your children. Next look at your outdoor space and see if those areas are explicitly represented and also consider where there might be opportunities to enhance other areas with more discreet resources to consolidate or expand the skill on which you are focusing. Then ask yourself the big question: what makes this activity outdoor play and not just indoor play taken outside? If, for example, you take your building bricks out onto a mat on a sunny day, that is not outdoor play. It is playing with indoor resources outside. If you have a water tray outdoors that is filled with the same equipment that you would have indoors then that also is not outdoor water play, it is your indoor water tray taken outside. The same rule applies to all areas of provision.

I am not saying that you shouldn't take indoor resources outside. For example, there might be occasions when you want to develop the 'indoor skills' but the children you are targeting want to be outside. So, rather than pull them in from their area of engagement, you would take those resources out. What I am saying is that you can't really call this 'outdoor play' in the sense of developing the skills that are unique to the outdoor environment.

Often I will work with settings that have huge wooden sand pits outdoors, but there is only four inches of sand in them and they are filled with exactly the same equipment as the indoor sand tray: we are back to indoor play outside, again.

In lots of outdoor play experiences there will be elements of indoor resourcing. These often act as a familiar 'bridge' that allow children to initially access familiar equipment that will lead them into other types of skill development. In your outdoor provision you should provide resources that will help children to make a link with or repeat skills that you have previously taught them. They can then use these skills to support them in their outdoor experience. But what have you got in the area that makes it 'outdoor provision'? Have you acknowledged the skill development that this outdoors area can offer and are you promoting it?

Thinking creatively

Take the time to work with your team to really ensure that everyone has an understanding of skill development in children and how effective use of the indoor or outdoor environment can have a significant impact on their attainment. Of course children's development, both indoors and out, is not purely linked to markers of academic attainment, although the current educational climate puts us under immense pressure to work purely to these academic goals.

One of the great joys of working in early years education is the opportunity to build children's imagination, language and ability to think creatively. As a practitioner, you will be able to promote all of these skills through the activities that you plan and the direct teaching opportunities that you create. But we should also be ensuring that we are giving children lots of open ended experiences in their continuous provision that allow them to discover, experiment and explore within the environment around them both inside and out.

Regular and rigorous assessment of children's command of vocabulary, types of talk used, strategies for problem solving and thinking skills will allow you to enhance your provision with resources and experiences that they can use to consolidate what they know and build their knowledge further.

One useful thing that you can do to help you to think about your environment in this way is to complete an environment plan for your classroom or each room within your setting. This example is taken from my book *From Vacant to Engaged* (Featherstone Education, 2012).

Environment Plan

Setting name

....

Year

....

Area	Skill	Exceeding	Expected	Emerging
Mark Making Area	Making representative marks	• Recognisable figures, objects and letters • Smaller and more controlled marks Resources	• Attempts to make recognisable figures, objects and letters with some features identifiable • Medium scale marks Resources	• Meaning attached to marks made • Some identifiable shapes • Large scale marks Resources
Workshop Area	Cutting	• Hold scissors correctly at all times • Cut round a template moving the paper effectively Resources	• Usually hold scissors correctly • Cuts up and along in a linear fashion Resources	• Begin to hold scissors correctly • Make random snips Resources
Construction	Joining and attaching	• Connecting different shapes and sizes of construction pieces in a variety of ways • Connecting small pieces together Resources	• Connecting medium sized pieces with some irregular shapes on top of and next to each other Resources	• Using regular shaped construction pieces on top of or next to each other Resources

An environment plan

Ideally you want children to feel free to move resources around the setting so they are not stuck in one place, but also you should be creating little pockets of experiences everywhere to enhance any 'moments' that arise. These would include, opportunities to mark make, problem solve and little baskets of books linked to an area of interest or play that will encourage the children to use books in a real situation. Practice should be multi-layered and skill development opportunities should appear in as many different guises as possible to give a higher chance of engagement.

I encourage all of the settings that I work with to complete an environment plan every year. It's a very simple document to put together but it's useful in clarifying with the team why their setting looks the way it does. It provides a clear link between assessment and the environment and it clearly shows how you have changed the environment in response to children's needs.

At the beginning of the year you can use your assessment to identify your key gaps. Once you have those as a priority list then you can arrange your setting (indoors and out) to reflect a heavier weighting in space and resourcing for your key areas of development. Now within all areas you look at the skills that you need to develop and make sure that there is enough appropriate resourcing to support that development. The environment plan is a way of recording all of this information. It should be done in bullet points and kept really simple.

There are of course lots of indoor enhancements that you can make to your outdoor provision such as books, mark making material and so on. But you are placing them in your outdoor provision to capitalise on children's interest and engagement in the outdoors. This engagement and interest will help with the job of developing basic skills like reading and writing. However, in theory (and still in some settings), those skills could be mastered in the classroom, without taking a step into the outside world!

If I am doing an outdoor project with a setting, I will get the staff to go around each of their outdoor areas, look at their resources and ask the question: what makes this outdoor?

So, to sum up:

- Start with assessment to identify need

- Reflect the need identified in the provision you offer

- Link 'bridging skills' to indoor provision

- Be clear and explicit about why you have put indoor provision outside (such as your water tray)

- Be clear and explicit about how you are planning for the development of outdoor skills

- Enhance your explicit outdoor provision with indoor provision (for example, mark making, reading, numeracy) for added engagement and basic skill development

Example of an environment plan

Section One: My space

Include photographs, pencil drawings, maps…whatever you feel most comfortable with that shows what your environment looks like (indoors and out).

Section Two: Autumn term set up

In this section, list all of your areas in turn and describe how, and more importantly, **WHY** you have set them up in the way that you have.

What you have set up should be driven by assessment of the CURRENT cohort. If you have no assessment of the children you will be getting, then go with your prior knowledge of other cohorts on point of entry and what you know about skill development in children.

You need to record something along these lines:

Area: Mark Making (indoor)

★ I have placed my mark making area next to my dough area as there are a number of activities for emergent mark makers that utilise elements of both areas.

★ There is a large clear floor area that allows for large-scale gross motor mark making as well as table top space for the development of fine motor work.

★ I have specifically chosen resources for the shelving that will meet the needs of the children – identified by their last assessment (see assessment file July 2012).

★ For my emergent mark makers I have...

★ To develop pincer grip I have...

★ For the development of fine motor movement I have...

★ I have included a photograph for reference...

This is a good activity for your whole team to do as it makes you ask yourself why you have a particular resource on the shelf. Also, don't be worried if your shelves look a little bit empty to start with (as long as you have a plan). You need to show children appropriate use of some equipment and often this means a staggered start to introducing resources that you have in mind.

Section Three: Spring term set up

In a different colour on your document show only the changes you have made in each area, stating why. Include a spring term photograph for reference.

Section Four: Summer term set up

As above – **SHOW** how you have made changes and **WHY**.

Section Five: Does it work?

The only way that you will know if your environment is working is to stand back and look at it. You need to regularly build opportunities into your timetable to do this. To get a really good picture of the areas of your setting that are working well, observations need to be done by a number of adults on a number of different occasions at different times of the day. These observations don't need to be pages and pages long – they just need to tell you what is working well and who is accessing what.

This is a quick environment observation I did in a reception/Year 1 setting.

I listed all of the areas/activities and then visited each one every 15 minutes. I used a tick if there were children in the area and then a 'b' for boys, 'g' for girls and 'm' for mixed. You can clearly see which areas are not being accessed. If this shows a pattern over time then you need to address that use of space.

Standing back and assessing is a crucial step which is often missed. When we are working with children we are often very involved in their play and we don't stand back and just look. Areas that provide high levels of engagement will always be well populated by children. You can see from one of these observations which areas are under-used but also if a particular gender group is dominating a specific space or activity. You can then amend your space or resourcing in response to your observations, assessments and children's preferences.

Areas in use

Workshop	✓g	✓m	✓m	✓m	✓m	✓m
Card making						
Medal painting	–	✓m	✓b	✓g	✓m	–
Maths table	✓	✓	✓	✓	–	✓
White board	✓	✓	✓	✓	✓	–
Outdoor	✓	✓	✓	✓	✓	✓
Role-play writing table (Central)	✓g	–	✓m	–	–	–
Computer	✓m	–	✓m	✓g	✓m	✓m
Role-play	–	–	–	–	✓b	–
Sand (bay)	–	–	–	✓g	–	–
Construction role-play	✓m	–	–	–	✓g	✓m
Letter formation area	–	–	–	–	–	–
Reading	–	–	–	–	–	–
Water (bay)	–	–	–	–	–	–

Outdoor

Farm play (real grass)	–	–	✓m	–	–	–
Maths (adult)	✓	✓	✓	✓	✓	✓
Reading (den)	✓	✓	✓	✓g	✓	✓
Sports day prac equipment	✓m	✓m	✓m	✓m	✓m	✓b
Tent with books	✓g	✓m	✓g	–	–	✓g
Home made skittles (adult)	✓	✓	✓	✓	✓	✓
Drawing (mark making table)	✓m	–	–	✓g	–	✓b
Garage	✓	✓	✓	✓	✓b	✓b
Shell exploration	–	–	–	–	–	–
Water play	✓b	–	–	–	–	✓g

Chapter 2

Planning for continuous provision

Every aspect of your continuous provision should be linked to the on-going assessment and observation of your current cohort. The size, shape and frequency of the areas you create along with the resources that you put into them should show that you are aware of the children's strengths and weaknesses in that particular area and what you are doing to support their learning.

Long term planning for continuous provision

Your long term planning for continuous provision should be based on your last summative assessment. When the children enter your setting you will spend a period of time assessing them against Development Matters. Once this assessment period is complete you will have the information that will tell you what areas of development your cohort (and individual children) are strongest in and those that need more support.

You would use this information as a starting point to plan how you were going to create an effective learning space.

Medium term planning for continuous provision

Once you have structured your environment indoors and out, you then need to make sure that the areas of provision that you have created are filled with appropriate resources that match the different stages of development that assessment has identified.

If you know that in terms of mark making, you have some children who are still very 'gross motor', some who are developing a smaller range of movement and some who are already beginning to triangulate and attempt to record recognisable letters then your mark making provision should contain resources that support every level of development and not just generic pencil and paper.

Short term planning for continuous provision

If you have used your summative assessment to help you to plan your areas and their contents, your on-going assessment and observations will help you to dress your resources to engage the children's interests and also enhance your provision in response to a learning need or the particular interests of a child or group of children.

It is great if you can link all of your areas to assessment, even better if you have resourced them to meet identified learning needs, but all of this planning will be ineffective if you can't get the children into the provision in the first place. Then, once they are in it, you need to encourage them to use the resources that were meant for them. This is where 'dressing' to children's interests comes into its own. Our observations of what children feel are significant. Events and characters (real and imagined) in their every day lives will be crucial in making links to quality learning in our continuous provision.

The EYFS guidance is very clear that there needs to be a good mix of adult directed teaching and child initiated learning in your setting. What it is not very clear on is how much of each there should be. The reason for this is there is no real definitive answer, as with a great deal of early years practice, it depends on a range of other factors.

Before you even begin to discuss percentages and ratios, the first thing you need to do is to define what you mean and understand by the terms 'adult directed' and 'child initiated'. I often find that these definitions can be tricky to clarify within a team and that practitioners' individual interpretations can differ considerably.

Direct teaching

The next thing I would do is to work out how you think your direct teaching is going to work because that is the easier bit.

- Is it going to be every day? If so, how many times?

- Are you going to teach the whole class or group by ability?

- Which members of the team will be planning and which will be delivering?

If you are following a programme such as Letters and Sounds or Read, Write Inc. how are you going to fit those in?

For example, you might decide that you are going to have three sessions of direct teaching each day. These will be at the beginning or the end of a session as you don't want to compromise the children's opportunities for sustained shared thinking, exploration and deep level learning. Great! That's sorted! The problem is what do you do when the children leave you after the direct teaching session?

Well you have a couple of options. Once you have finished the direct teaching you might say 'red group you stay with me and the rest of you go and get busy!' What a shame for red group having to do more 'work' while everyone else gets to go and 'play'. Still I am sure that they will give you maximum engagement, after all who wouldn't rather count multilink as opposed to playing in the water tray? Once 'red group' have finished their task with you, your next dilemma is what to do next. Most practitioners opt for developing a common condition known as 'tambourine elbow', this is common in early years practitioners and members of the Salvation Army and occurs from excessive shaking of the tambourine to indicate a change in activity!

So, red group have finished and while their seats are still warm you reach for the tambourine and shake it. Everything, (well, nearly everything) stops. All the creativity, all of the sustained shared thinking, problem solving, deep level learning, imaginative play, everything! You then proceed with the 'I am looking for blue group mantra'. Now depending on the genetic make up of blue group, this could take some time.

After five minutes you have managed to round up four of the six children, but two are still AWOL: probably outside on the bikes or making guns. Telling them that if they don't come in now they will never go out again, probably does nothing for their levels of engagement but at least you have managed to rally blue group, safe in the knowledge that in approximately 15 minutes the tambourine will come out again and the herding of green group will begin!

I don't think anyone would argue against the fact that there needs to be some direct teaching in early years. Maybe with my idealist head on I would argue that every aspect of the EYFS can be taught through quality play based learning, but with my realist head on I know that in the majority of settings that type of learning just isn't practical and nor does it fit in with the way most settings operate.

My issue with grouping children for literacy, mathematics and then 'topic', is that the groups are too broad. At this stage of children's development they can excel and need support with different aspects of the same subject area. So a child might be a brilliant talker but not such an adept mark maker yet they will be in the same literacy group for both. Another might be fantastic at shape but not so great with numbers but again will be in the same mathematics group for both.

I know what some of you are thinking. How could you possibly have a different group for each aspect of each subject area that you teach? The answer for me is ... don't have groups! When I say 'don't group your children', what I mean is that you would group them in the aspect of the subject that you were planning to teach. Then (and this is the good bit) you take the next steps to the children not bring the children to you.

For example, you might do a direct phonics, literacy and mathematics teaching session every day. You would always place these at the beginning or end of a continuous provision session. You might ability group the children or teach them as a whole class. At the end of this direct teaching session your children all go into continuous provision.

WARNING: When I say continuous provision, I of course mean provision that is linked to assessment, levelled and dressed for attainment. Not just play areas.

Objective-led planning

I have been working with Halton Lodge Primary School (Runcorn) where reception teacher Ruth and her team have been trialing the objective-led planning system. This is the planning that she was using:

So, you might happen across a group of mixed ability children setting up an ice cream shop in the role-play area (this happened to me in Durham). If they were engaged in some amazing play or learning you would forget your objective-led planning sheet and observe/assess/support what was going on.

If their play is fairly low level and non-challenging (which it often can be) then you would go in, play alongside and then introduce the need for some kind of writing such as a menu, a sign, a brochure, a website. Once you have engendered some enthusiasm, you match your resources and your expectations to the ability of the children and the next steps objectives.

You do not turn it into a 'red group' table top session! You are going for high level engagement so you need to keep it relevant to their play and not hijack their play with your planning agenda. If it feels like it is going that way then drop it and pick it up again at another time in another place. It really is the most effective way of teaching within the principles of the EYFS and more than that, it allows you to be creative, have some fun and really 'teach' rather than just 'deliver'.

Of course the key to the effectiveness of this planning is how you plan your day and the role of the other adults that are working with the children.

Chapter 3

Timetabling continuous provision

Although no two settings have exactly the same timetable, there are similarities that exist wherever I go. As I have previously said, there needs to be a good balance between adult lead and child initiated teaching and learning. In the current climate I tend to find that there is a very strong leaning towards adult led delivery. This is because this style of teaching puts the adult very much in control and makes tracking input and evidence very easy, although it is not always the best model for learning.

Undoubtedly there has to be some direct teaching in early years, especially with regard to children's acquisition of the basic skills of literacy and numeracy. Having said that, there has to be a balance. As early years practitioners, we know what is appropriate for the stage of development of our children and should keep that firmly in mind if we are being asked to jump onto the latest literacy or numeracy bandwagon that will have our children sitting on the carpet 'chanting' for ridiculously long periods of time.

Assessment is the most important tool that we have got at our disposal for guiding us on what to teach and when to teach it. If children are *not ready* for a particular stage of learning then we should be using our resources to help to prepare them. If they are *more than ready* then we should take them to the next step on their learning journey.

There is no such thing as the 'perfect timetable'. Timetables will change as the needs of the children change. Also in lots of larger settings you do not have the luxury of complete freedom with your timetables due to other restrictions that are imposed upon you, over which you have no control, such as assembly or ICT time. Everyone's timetable will be different and you have to do the best with what you have got.

After working with a number of settings, over a number of years, to support them in implementing objective-led planning within the restrictions of their timetable, the example that follows is a generic template that I have come up with. It has had to be 'tweaked' by each individual setting that has used it, but it might give you a starting point to get you going.

Obviously, at the beginning of the year, or for a new intake it would be very different as children will be getting used to you and your setting. Ultimately what we are aiming for is a timetable with a lot of fluidity and the minimum amount of breaks.

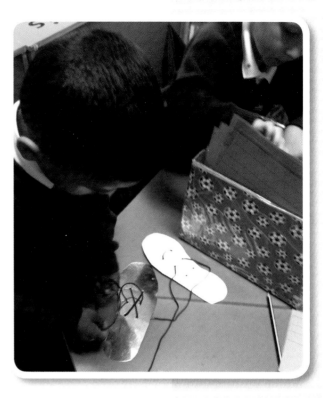

At the beginning of the year you undoubtedly have a timetable that reflects the opposite. You would be doing lots of stopping and starting to help children to be clear about how to use your space appropriately with lots of very public displays of delight when they are successful.

At the point you are introducing this sort of timetable you will have already:

- structured your environment around needs identified by your last summative assessment and ongoing observations

- levelled your continuous provision in each area linked to assessment

- dressed some of your continuous provision for interest

- created opportunities for exploration, problem solving and thinking

Within this timetable there are going to be:

- opportunities for direct teaching

- opportunities for teaching through continuous provision using objective-led planning

- opportunities to observe, assess and support children's learning

- time to talk to children and find out what interests and motivates them

Start of the day

Self registration

At the beginning of the session I am a huge fan of self registration and have had great success with children from the age of two years and upwards being able to successfully self register. The reason that I like it so much is not just because it helps to develop children's independence and self reliance, it also frees up adults to interact and support learning rather than go through the ineffective and over rehearsed routines of days of the week and the weather. If I have just walked in from the outside, why would I want to sit and wait for the VIP to wander over to the window and assess the climate while you whip out your Velcro weather chart?

Always remember that attainment is directly linked to engagement. How much attainment is happening during your morning carpet session?

Continuous provision short session

This is a short session of continuous provision that takes place while the children are arriving and self registering. It didn't exist in my first versions of this timetable but was introduced in response to a need identified mainly by reception teachers in schools.

The continuous provision here is not throughout the whole space but is usually just table top and is game or play based. It can be linked to an area of development identified by assessment. So, if you know that your children have a particular area of development such as problem solving, then this session of continuous provision could be entirely linked to that. When this is the case, I would plan a weekly focus and have the same activities out every day for that week.

This session has also been used very successfully as a time to hear readers. Rather than pulling children out of learning through their longer continuous provision sessions, this session is used every day for an adult to hear individual or guided reading. The number of adults that you have available and the length of the session will dictate the number of readers that you can hear.

As the same provision is going to be available at this time all week then children are not as likely to 'miss an opportunity' if they are asked to go and read.

Adult role

This session can only work if there are a minimum of two adults. One adult will welcome the children and facilitate the self registration and access to the continuous provision. The other adult will be doing some direct input such as hearing readers or speech and language intervention.

All together: interest session

This is a daily session where everyone comes together on the carpet to talk. During this session children will have the opportunity to discuss the things that are important to them and also adults will be able to introduce ideas and concepts to children as well as signposting learning opportunities that are available that day.

It is from this session that you will record children's interests and then use that information to shape your planning and provision.

Teaching children to talk

I would always have a weekly talk focused on the type of talk that assessment had identified that the children needed to develop. I would record this 'talk focus' on my weekly planning and also indicate any key vocabulary that I felt the children needed to develop in relation to it. This way you are showing how you are using assessment to identify need and then how you are planning to meet that need.

Talk is a fantastic tool for early years practitioners and holds the key to unlock every aspect of learning, but talk isn't just about talking! There are many different types of talk and language and children should have lots of opportunity to experience and practice all of them.

Through quality planned talk sessions children should experience all of the following and more.

Talk for:

- social interaction – building relationships

- making choices and decisions, developing curiosity

- developing language – using familiar and newly introduced vocabulary

- developing communication and negotiation skills

- expressing emotions and feelings

- recalling own experience

- developing mathematical language and concepts in a meaningful context

- developing day to day activities like cooking

- communicating ideas in construction of props

- projecting themselves into feelings, actions of others

- taking on a role in an imaginary situation, both real and fantasy

- conflict resolution, both real and imaginary

- problem-solving in real and imaginary situations

- tidying up! – talk for negotiation, organisation

- comparison

- cooperation and collaboration, beginning to work as part of a group

- sharing and turn taking

- naming of familiar objects

- the development of descriptive language

- positional language

- naming attributes of common objects and animals

- developing an awareness of a real life environment that is different from their own

- communicating emotion e.g. fear

- discussing previous experiences that were good

- description and exploration of colour, texture, shape and size of objects found in real and imaginary habitats

- awareness of danger

- recognition of 'sameness' and 'difference'

- finding out about past events in their own lives and the lives of others

- making choices

- organising ideas and experiences

- expressing feelings and ideas

To ensure that children are getting lots of opportunities for talk development, a talk focus should be part of your weekly planning. Use your assessments and observations to identify which areas of talk development that children are weakest in and then focus on those in your teaching times and interactions.

It is not enough just to *speak*, we have to teach children to talk. In the revised EYFS document what was Communication, Language and Literacy has now been sub-sectioned into the prime areas of Communication and Language (which covers listening and attention, understanding and speaking) and the specific area of Literacy (which covers reading and writing).

If you use the age related descriptors for Communication and Language, they give you a very comprehensive reference point, not only for the type of talk activity that you should be planning, but also the national expectation for age related attainment.

Communication and Language
(from Development Matters, DfES 2012)

22–36 months

- Uses language as a powerful means of widening contacts, sharing feelings experiences and thoughts.

- Holds a conversation, jumping from topic to topic.

- Learns new words very rapidly and is able to use them in communicating.

- Uses gestures, sometimes with limited talk, e.g. reaches toward toy, saying 'I have it'.

- Uses a variety of questions (e.g. what, where, who).

- Uses simple sentences (e.g. 'Mummy gonna work.')

- Beginning to use word endings (e.g. going, cats)

30–50 months

- Beginning to use more complex sentences to link thoughts (e.g. using, and, because).

- Can retell a simple past event in correct order (e.g. went down slide, hurt finger).

- Uses talk to connect ideas, explain what is happening and anticipate what might happen next, recall and relive past experiences.

- Questions why things happen and gives explanations. Asks e.g. who, what, when, how.

- Uses a range of tenses (e.g. play, playing, will play, played).

- Uses intonation, rhythm and phrasing to make the meaning clear to others.

- Uses vocabulary focused on objects and people that are of particular importance to them.

- Builds up vocabulary that reflects the breadth of their experiences.

- Uses talk in pretending that objects stand for something else in play, e.g 'This box is my castle.'

40–60+ months

- Extends vocabulary, especially by grouping and naming, exploring the meaning and sounds of new words.

- Uses language to imagine and recreate roles and experiences in play situations.

- Links statements and sticks to a main theme or intention.

- Uses talk to organise, sequence and clarify thinking, ideas, feelings and events.

- Introduces a storyline or narrative into their play

Early Learning Goal

Children express themselves effectively, showing awareness of listeners' needs. They use past, present and future forms accurately when talking about events that have happened or are to happen in the future. They develop their own narratives and explanations by connecting ideas or events

The range of talk skills that children are able to develop are quite diverse and complex and these are far in advance of what they are expected to record in their writing.

Literacy
writing

22–36 months

- Distinguishes between the different marks they make

30–50 months

- Sometimes gives meaning to marks as they draw and paint.

- Ascribes meanings to marks that they see in different places

40–60+ months

- Gives meaning to marks they make as they draw, write and paint.

- Begins to break the flow of speech into words.

- Continues a rhyming string.

- Hears and says the initial sound in words.

- Can segment the sounds in simple words and blend them together.

- Links sounds to letters, naming and sounding the letters of the alphabet.

- Uses some clearly identifiable letters to communicate meaning, representing some sounds correctly and in sequence.

- Writes own name and other things such as labels, captions.

- Attempts to write short sentences in meaningful contexts

Early Learning Goal

Children use their phonic knowledge to write words in ways which match their spoken sounds. They also write some irregular common words. They write simple sentences which can be read by themselves and others. Some words are spelt correctly and others are phonetically plausible.

The previous list is a really useful reference for looking at what 'next steps' for talk might look like in your planning, but also for mapping your coverage of types of talk and use of language.

I wouldn't expect you to say 'right children, this week we are going to focus on talk for conflict resolution and here is some key vocabulary that I want you to use'! But if you have planned for a weekly talk focus and all of the adults in the setting are aware of what it is and the key vocabulary then you would take opportunities to support it as they arose.

To support this daily interests session, I would have an 'interests board' where I could display ideas that the children have had or things that they have brought in from home that have promoted interaction and discussion.

This sort of display also makes it really easy to track how children's interests are used in provision to promote high level engagement.

Adult role

If there are two adults, then one will lead the session while the other 're-sets' the environment after the first session of continuous provision. As this is not a taught session then it is a legitimate use of the other adult's time to set up the provision for the next session. They can join the discussion as soon as the set up is complete.

Dough Gym/Funky Fingers time

Every day the children need to engage in some sort of intervention that is going to help them to develop their gross and fine motor skills as well as their sense of balance, coordination and proprioception.

For the children who need more gross motor development then they can work with an adult on an initiative like Dough Gym. The following excerpts are taken from my book *Getting Ready to Write* (Featherstone Education 2013).

What is Dough Gym?

- Dough Gym is a gym for children where you work out with dough – simple!

- Dough Gym is a specific daily intervention – to have impact it has to be regular and consistent.

- Dough Gym is exclusive – you need to make the children who need this intervention feel special and chosen for all of the right reasons, not just because they are failing. I usually work with a maximum of eight children, not a whole group.

- Dough Gym is planned – this initiative is about targeting specific areas of development. It won't work if you just slap a bit of dough around!

- Dough Gym is done to music – I have found that this is key to its success. Children are highly engaged by music and the beat is crucial when it comes to performing the Dough Gym moves. Choose your music carefully. Something that is popular and current is far more likely to get high levels of engagement than working out to 'Jesus' hands were kind hands'!

How does a session work?

Dough Gym needs to take place at the beginning or end of a session so that you are not pulling children out of continuous provision or away from areas of interest and exploration. I always prefer to do mine at the beginning of the day. As you want Dough Gym to carry a bit of prestige and have the 'envyability factor' it is better if it is done in your main space and that children aren't taken off to another room to do it! You can run Dough Gym and Funky Fingers at the same time so that all children are having a daily intervention that is supporting and extending their gross and fine motor development.

To start, the Dough Gym children present you with their membership cards and then take up their places. It is important that the children stand, as part of this initiative is to develop their balance, posture, proprioception, hand-eye coordination and bilateral movement which is less effective when you sit down.

Children's backs need to be straight and their feet shoulder width apart. They will find it very tempting to bend forward thus using their back rather than their shoulders and arms to support the dough. I always tell mine to squeeze their bottoms as this tightens the 'core' and helps prevent bending

When the music starts, begin with shoulder pivots and arm stretches utilising the biggest range of movement interspersed with wrist, hand and finger exercises. Use the dough for resistance work: anything from squashing it with a flat palm and a straight arm to pinching small bits out of it. The large ball of dough is also useful for developing arm muscles and pivots by lifting, as well as hand arches and finger pivots by squeezing.

The session should be fast paced and hard work but most of all fun. You want to keep the children coming back for more. The role of the Dough Gym leader is quite like that of a slightly crazed aerobics instructor. Once the children become familiar with a few basic moves then you will be able to sequence them just by calling out the name of the move when you want the children to change. As the children become more proficient, you can add more moves and create a more complex and challenging work out.

Funky Fingers

As I have previously said, there is no point in just getting children to squash a few bits of dough in time to music if it not going to have any impact on their fine motor development. So the first port of call is assessment: you need to know where the children are currently in terms of their dexterity and then identify what the next steps are.

To do this assessment, you need to take into account a child's grip with a variety of objects of different sizes and also their ability to use their fingers, or manipulate apparatus or resources to pick up small objects. Then you can use this information to create activities that will challenge and extend the children.

When it comes to Funky Fingers activities, the speed at which you ask the children to perform the activity or the number of times you ask them to complete the task in a given time frame can really increase the level of challenge.

Sometimes you will get a group of children whose dexterity is amazing, they could pick up a speck of dust with one eye closed! For these children I usually organise some sort of activity that you can do to music which is linked to the principles of brain gym. One setting I have worked with does a very effective brain gym Zumba with lots of cross body, bi-lateral movements and a couple of maracas thrown in for good measure!

How would a Funky Fingers session work?

One group of children will be working with an adult having a Dough Gym session. The rest of the children will be split into groups identified by your assessment of their need and stage of development. With two adults it is advisable to have no more than five groups in total (including Dough Gym).

For example:

Group 1 – **Dough Gym**

Group 2 – **Pompoms and tweezers**

Group 3 – **Threading on skewers**

Group 4 – **Spiders in jelly**

Group 5 – **Zumba**

> Role of the adult:
> In this session the adult is either leading a specific group or supervising a number of groups.

An adult would need to be stationed with the Dough Gym and the Zumba children as they need direct input and will be following constant instruction. The other groups have a task to complete:

Group 2: How many pompoms can you move from the pot to the egg box with the tweezers?

Group 3: How fast can you fill the skewer with beads and then empty it again?

I tend to do my Dough Gym and Funky Fingers at the same time every day, usually after the children have had a 'sitting' time, like carpet time or a direct teaching session. Everyone should know where their Funky Fingers group is and on your command they should take their places! Put the music on and everyone is working at the same time. You will be amazed how tiring working with dough and pompoms can be!

The Funky Fingers activities stay for a week and they are only used at Funky Fingers time and not as part of continuous provision. This helps you to ensure that you can really monitor how the children are using the activities to make sure they have ultimate impact, it also stops the children from getting bored with them.

The easiest way I have found for managing your Funky Fingers time is to have your activities in a box or on a tray under the table each morning. While one adult is finishing the carpet session then another can easily lift the resources out onto the table tops, or you can get the children to do it at the beginning of the session. Once the session is over the boxes can go back under the table out of the way.

Virtual Base time 1

Virtual base times are your adult directed taught time. They will happen daily and there will be up to three a day depending on the age and ability of your children. In most of the settings I work with, they are usually based around phonics, mathematics and literacy but it could be a taught input about anything.

Why are they called Virtual Bases?

For me the essence of good early years teaching is that it is done through children's interests and promotes high level engagement. Often this principle gets completely overlooked when it comes to carpet based teaching.

The 'base' in 'Virtual Base' just means a place to gather – it is the 'virtual' bit which is crucial. I called them this to remind practitioners that they shouldn't base their teaching in just one spot (usually the carpet) but that they should try and move around their space and teach in different places. This is good for two main reasons: one, it helps to maintain levels of engagement for children; two, it promotes teaching through other areas of learning and through other areas of the environment.

For example, if my focus for teaching in mathematics was counting, rather than get out the multilink and the white bears on the carpet, I might take my group of children into the music area. There I would get out the instruments and talk about how we play them 'appropriately', give them their correct names and then I might play two lots of beats, get the child to add them in their head and play the answer back to me.

It is the same concept as the multilink just delivered through music. Now, I appreciate that this is not the same as children having the opportunity to explore tone and pitch and so on but it does provide them with the knowledge and skills to be able to go on and do just that.

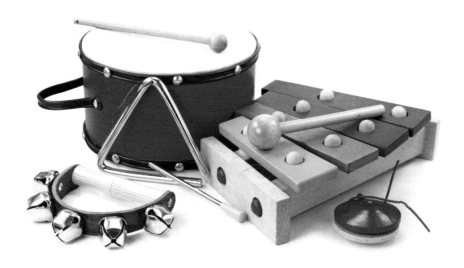

Virtual Bases work better the smaller the group of children. Obviously it would be impossible to fit 30 children in your block area or around your workshop table! If you can group your children by their development or ability then this can make your teaching input far more focused.

> Role of the adult:
> To deliver a planned objective to a designated group of children through other areas of the environment and other areas of learning.

WARNING: If you are going to ability group your children, make sure that within each group there are both higher and lower abilities to support aspirational learning and peer tutoring. If you split purely by ability you might find that your teaching is like trying to wade through treacle with some groups! If that is the case, it is not their fault – it is yours!

If your other adults are not comfortable or able to take a group then make sure they are supporting you directly during your teaching. Are they sitting with a designated group to give further questioning or support? They should definitely not be carrying out 'housekeeping' duties or sitting on a chair at the side of the carpet while you are teaching.

This Virtual Base usually lasts between 10 and 25 minutes depending on the age of the children and their stage of development. If you have got different adults working in different areas of the environment then this allows different groups to have Virtual Base times of different lengths. If I had a group of children who were at the stage of needing more time to complete an extended piece of writing then I could 'keep' my Virtual Base group working for a little while longer while the others finished and moved into continuous provision.

Continuous provision session 1

The children leave their Virtual Bases and the adults move with them into continuous provision. At this point the adults would pick up their objective-led planning focus as they will be looking for opportunities to deliver that alongside observing, assessing and generally supporting children's interests.

What adults must not do is to pick up their objective-led planning and approach it like a tick list, hunting children down! This planning had been put in place to support learning and provide extra focus for attainment, not to dominate learning at all costs.

You are probably going to run one more Virtual Base time before lunch (if it is appropriate for the age and stage of development of your children) so this session of continuous provision should last until then.

Brief tidy up

This is not a complete environment overhaul but a brief 're-set' that will allow the following base time to be effective.

> **Role of the adult:**
> To support children's learning and development both indoors and out using the differentiated provision and objective-led planning.

Virtual Base time 2

This is your second direct teach of the day (if appropriate). The base time should run under the same principles as before just with a different teaching focus.

Assess and review

At the end of this base time it is a great opportunity to gather together and have a brief assess and review session where the children can have the opportunity to talk about what they have done.

Toilet, hand wash, home/lunch

If you are a sessional setting then you would just repeat the morning again.

Afternoon registration

This can be a quick whip through the register, a self registration and then meet on the carpet or a repeat of the morning self registration where the staff have the opportunity to hear more children read or carry out interventions.

Assess and review session

This is an opportunity to meet together on the carpet to talk about what the children have done so far that day and signpost possible learning opportunities for the afternoon.

Virtual Base time 3

This is your third and final direct teach of the day (if appropriate). The base time should run under the same principles as before just with a different teaching focus.

Continuous provision session 2

The children leave their Virtual Bases and the adults move with them into continuous provision. At this point, the adults would pick up their objective-led planning focus as they will be looking for opportunities to deliver that alongside observing, assessing and generally supporting children's interests.

As before, what adults must not do is to pick up their objective-led planning and approach it like a tick list, hunting children down! This planning had been put in place to support learning and provide extra focus for attainment, not to dominate learning at all costs.

Tidy up time

This is your tidy up at the end of the day. Hopefully this slot will get shorter the better children get at helping you to tidy up!

Carpet session

I like a decent carpet session at the end of the day where you can pull everything together, swap some stories about how your day has been and then enjoy a good book and a song before the rush to get coats. When you are building in timings to your timetable, try and make some decent provision for both talk and story at the end of the day.

> **Role of the adult:**
> To support children's learning and development both indoors and out using the differentiated provision and objective-led planning.

Snack, playtime and physical education

Three things that don't feature in this timetable are snack time, playtime and physical education (PE).

As I have previously said, we are trying to achieve constancy and flow in children's learning with as few breaks as possible, as a result we need to look carefully at all of the aspects of our practice and provision that cause these learning breaks and then evaluate them for their impact on attainment.

Snack time

When we provide snack time for children, what is it for and why are we doing it? There are many aspects of learning and social interaction that can be developed during snack, but usually only if there is an adult there to facilitate them. Snack is a great opportunity to develop language and social interaction, but if children have limited vocabulary and social skills, then they are not going to interact with each other. These skills will not develop on their own.

By the same token, you do not want an adult posted at the snack table all day every day. You need a happy medium. So you need to treat snack like any other area of continuous provision.

The first question you need to ask yourself is: what is it for?

- If it is to develop children's independence then how are we facilitating that? Can they cut up their own fruit, butter their own bread or wash their own dishes?

- If it is for social interaction, do we have an adult who has this as their objective to develop that week (in all areas not just snack)?

- Is it to develop talk? If so, then what have we put into our snack area to promote and inspire children's talk? Have you got unusual objects or photographs on the snack table for children to look at and talk about when there is no adult present?

Having some sort of focus on your snack table also means that an adult doesn't have to be there all of the time. They can just direct the children to look at whatever is there or 'model' the beginning of a conversation or discussion and then leave the children to it.

Once your rules and routines for snack are in place they should act as a facilitator for essential learning supported by appropriate adult intervention, not a chimps' tea party or an adult dominated space that takes away any or all opportunities for high level independence.

Playtime

The EYFS guidance talks about 'continuous outdoor access' and the philosophy behind this is that children can not only have access to learning in a completely unique environment, but that they will also be able to continue their learning indoors and out without breaks. If you have access to an outdoor space then there is no need for your children to stop everything and go out into the playground. Apart from the time that it takes to get coats on and off it makes a significant break in children's learning opportunities, interrupts the continuousness of continuous provision and reduces opportunities for objective-led planning.

I usually ask staff to try and equate learning and attainment to continuous outdoor provision and then do the same thing to playtime. Keep the one that has the greatest impact on children's learning.

PE

PE is a National Curriculum subject, but there is no legal requirement for children in early years to do it. Having said that, there are lots of unique and fun experiences that you can have in the hall with the PE apparatus that you will not get in exactly the same way outside. I think that it is worth having a couple of hall slots booked in on the timetable, but use them as an when you feel it is appropriate.

How many times have you spent the entire PE session getting children to take their socks and shoes off only to have to put them back on again because your allotted time is over? If you wait another half term then lots of the children will be far more dexterous and able to disrobe, meaning you get more done!

Chapter 4

Skill development in continuous provision

We should all be on a constant quest to ensure that quality learning is taking place for all children in our setting. This is very hard to do in an EYFS environment, which, although packed with potential, is also packed with unlimited opportunities for children to stagnate in low level activities that challenge no one.

If you want to do the 'stagnation test' for your setting and provision then pick a child and track them when they go into continuous provision. Every five minutes find them and write down exactly what they are doing. After an hour or so have a look at your list and then try to attach attainment for that child to the activity in which they were taking part.

If you have an able and articulate reception child that goes into the sand area and makes sand pies with a bucket and spade for 10 minutes, you have got to ask yourself:

Was this a new experience?

No.

Were they compliant?

Yes.

Were they engaged?

Possibly.

Were they learning?

Probably not.

If this pattern repeats itself a number of times for a number of children
then you have got a problem on your hands, especially if the children
are compliant! Some will be happy to sit in your snack, mark making or
construction area for 30 or 40 minutes getting on quietly, but producing
something that they could have done this time last term or last year. Partly
this will be because children like to make self affirming familiar choices and
partly because the provision has not been set up for skill development, so
even if an adult did intervene and try to promote more effective learning
the planning and resources are not in place to make that a very easy task.

Once your initial point of entry assessment is done, you will then be able
to set up your environment based on what this assessment has told you.
Within that environment you will have areas of continuous provision that will provide children
with lots of opportunities to think and explore but that will also be linked to next steps
development and then 'dressed' to children's interests. Even with all of this excellent provision
in place, stagnation can still come calling on a fairly regular basis.

There are key areas of any setting where this is most likely to strike: sand; water; malleable
materials; small world play; construction; role-play; music and movement; workshop and
paint. So what can save these areas from stagnating? Skill development!

When I am planning for my areas of provision I always have a list of the 'types' of resources
that I am going to offer as basic provision. I don't list each item individually but give an
overview by type. I call this list my non-negotiables. Then, each week I choose three or four
areas where I know that it is easy for children to revert to low level non challenging play and I
plan for development in a specific skill.

Wet sand

- development of manipulative skills (filling the bucket, turning it over, making a sand castle)

- talk about sizes of the buckets and spades

- match large spade to large bucket

- match colours (red spade to red bucket)

- match the sand castle to the bucket

- develop vocabulary (full, empty, nearly full)

- respond to instructions (Can you fill the bucket? Can you make a sand castle?)

- talk about their experiences of sand play (beach, sand pit)

- count sand castles

- talk about the best size of spade to fill the bucket (large spade and large bucket)

- share equipment and space

- making shapes in a confined space

- talk about the shapes, describing them, comparing them, counting them

- recognise and name shapes

- match the shape to the mould

- compare the sizes of spoons, ladles and scoops (large/small, heavy/light)

- count sand shapes

- develop social skills (share equipment and materials; take turns; cooperating with each other

- be aware and able to describe the properties and texture of damp/wet sand develop descriptive vocabulary (wet, cold, damp, hard, soft, smooth, rough, bumpy)

- experience the therapeutic nature of playing with sand

- develop fine motor skills to facilitate pre-writing

- develop independence in putting on aprons

- develop manipulative skills (filling the bucket, turning it over, making sand castles)

- investigate if it is possible to make a sand castle using the various shapes of containers

- discuss why it works/does not work

- compare the shapes made

- explore and represent familiar objects in 3D form

- recognise and name basic shapes

- link sand play to a nursery rhyme (such as Jack and Jill)

- develop one-to-one correspondence

- development of manipulative skills (filling shapes, turning them over and making sand shapes)

- demonstrate concept of area

- recognise and create patterns

- develop vocabulary (describing what they are doing, describing the patterns they make)

- identify name and describe the natural materials and the patterns they make

- describe the patterns

- compare the patterns made with different objects

- share sand space

- recognise and name parts of the body

- explore shape and form

- name objects

- develop observational skills

- recognise that damp sand holds impressions

- demonstrate simple sequencing

- use comparative language (heavy/light, long/short, wide/narrow, tall/small)

- predict which containers hold most/least sand

- take part in small world role-play

- explore and recognise features of the natural world through sand and enhancements

- identify equipment

- talk about what they are making (giving likes and dislikes)

- compare the sizes of bowls, spoons, cups

- develop comparative language

- share and agree on the props and the story line

- re-tell a story in sequence

- design and create environments for their stories

Water

- talk about their experiences at bath-time, at the beach, the swimming pool, washing dishes, washing clothes

- name toys and equipment

- respond to instructions (Can you fill the cup, teapot? Can you pour the water from the jug to the cup?)

- share equipment and space

- discuss and recognise the need for rules (no splashing)

- develop the therapeutic nature of playing with warm water

- experience properties of water, investigate surface tension

- develop manipulative skills (filling cups, yogurt cartons and pouring out)

- develop concentration skills

- find out that some objects float

- discover that not all heavy things sink/all light things float

- predict which objects will float/sink

- observe how some objects that look alike behave differently (golf ball/table tennis ball)

- make comparisons between objects that float and objects that sink

- explore water in relation to weather (rain, ice, snow)

- develop vocabulary associated with weather

- describe the weather

- recognise the need for appropriate clothing and equipment

- develop vocabulary (full, empty, nearly full, holds more, pour, flow)

- experience and explore the nature and properties of water

- develop descriptive vocabulary (wet, warm, cold, hot, splash, gurgle, trickle, swish, drip)

- develop fine motor skills to facilitate pre-writing

- recognise and create patterns

- develop vocabulary (describing what they are doing, describing the patterns they make)

- develop descriptive language (wavy, straight, ripples, circles)

- begin to use comparative language precisely (full/empty, wide/narrow, wet/dry, heavy/light)

- predict which container holds most/least

- observe how water finds its own level

- observe how different objects behave in water

- begin to discover that water can exist in different states

- investigate absorbency

- develop relevant language (drip on/through, fall to bits, go through, roll off/run off, soak in/up, stay dry)

- discover that water can exist in different states

- investigate ice and discover some of its features

- develop appropriate vocabulary (freeze, melt, frozen, change, colder, icy, slippery, frosty, hard)

- investigate condensation on windows

- develop early concepts of forces and energy

- examine water pressure

- develop early experience of volume

- understand that the largest funnel empties first

Malleable materials

- develop manipulative/motor skills

- discover the properties of the dough (talk about properties)

- cooperate/share/collaborate

- enjoyment/develop sensory experiences

- self expression

- relieve frustration

- language about length (comparison)

- model

- shape

- aesthetic awareness

- identify colours and develop appropriate language

- develop sensory experiences

- enjoyment

- develop discussion and description of materials

- develop of rolling skills

- develop observation skills

- talk about textures, imprints in the flat dough

- flatten dough

- imaginative play (make buns, cakes)

- develop manipulative skills

- develop language

- language development (describing marks and patterns)

- share equipment/collaboration

- prediction

- compare and share

- develop concept of heavy and light

- develop concept of balancing and equal weights

- language development describing squeezed and shaped dough

- creative/imaginative development

- discuss, cooperate, have fun and enjoy dough

- develop representational skills

- develop creative/imaginative skills and ideas

- incorporate into role-play area

Creative (music)

- explore and recognise how sounds can be changed

- sing simple songs from memory

- recognise repeated sounds and sound patterns

- listen with discrimination, to develop pitch discrimination

- develop an awareness that sounds and music can be interpreted through movement

- develop language to describe sounds, movement, body positions

- express and communicate ideas, thoughts and feelings by using a variety of songs and musical instruments

- use imagination in music

- respond in a variety of ways to what they see, hear, smell, touch and feel

- express and communicate ideas, thoughts and feelings by using movement

- match movements to music

- use their imagination in movement and dance

Workshop

- learn about the different ways in which materials can be joined

- learn to cut

- embellish designs and creations

- review their work and then revisit it to make changes

- extend ideas and logical thinking

- develop fine motor skills

- cooperate and collaborate

- learn about space, shape, area, estimation, symmetry

- design and make using a variety of materials and techniques

- gain knowledge of the properties of various materials

- explore colour, shape, texture, form and space in 2D

- express and communicate ideas, thoughts and feelings by using a wide range of materials, suitable tools

- use imagination in art and design

- respond in a variety of ways to what they see, touch, feel and hear

Paint

- explore colour, shape, texture, form and space in 2D and 3D

- express and communicate ideas, thoughts and feelings by using a wide range of materials and suitable tools

- use imagination in art and design

- respond in a variety of ways to the senses

- differentiate marks and movements on paper

- work creatively on a small and large scale

- experiment to create different textures

- explore and experiment using a range of senses

- use one object to represent another

- respond to comments and questions, entering into dialogue about the creations

Outdoor play: wheeled toys

The thrill, the will and the skill

One of the biggest outdoor play frustrations that I come across in settings is boys on wheeled toys. Their need for speed seems to frustrate and perplex practitioners in equal measure, often resulting in a 'bike ban' when all of the offending items are locked away until further notice!

That of course is one solution and it does remove the immediate symptom, what it doesn't do however, is tackle the cause and it denies other children the opportunities to use the wheeled toys. Plus we all know that the offending children never come back to you and say, 'As a result of the sanction that you have imposed, I have considered the inappropriateness of my actions with regard to the bicycles and I can assure you I have seen the error of my ways and will never do it again!' They just get frustrated and cause disturbance and disruption elsewhere.

If we look at the use of wheeled toys in settings in terms of skill development then this can often help us to find a better solution. As I have said, you can look at skill development as a physical and a cognitive concept. Alongside their potential to develop children's physical skill we can use wheeled toys to look at forces, speed, direction, instruction, number recognition, reading, the list is huge! If we ask ourselves 'what do children develop physically' from the use of wheeled toys then the skills list we come up with is often very emergent. It is good for developing balance, proprioception, coordination and lower body strength but if you are working with children beyond the age of two years, are these really the skills your children are lacking?

When we the look at the children using the wheeled toys and apply the development criteria to them, are they just getting the hang of balance and coordination? Are the wheeled toys that we have on offer providing a level of physical challenge? Or can they race around the outdoor area at 90 miles an hour? (Turning a corner on two wheels and nearly taking out two well behaved girls and a teaching assistant!)

If the answer is the latter, then the wheeled toys are not actually providing any level of real physical challenge and in that respect they are not appropriate provision. They are being used for one very different and powerful reason: thrill! The children that I watch constantly crashing into each other while going around the track don't do it because they lack coordination, they do it because it is exciting, fun and full of risk.

The reason that children will be so eager to jump on the wheeled toys as opposed to anything else is because of that thrill factor. The hard truth is, that for them, there is nothing else in your environment that holds the same level of excitement, engagement or risk. By comparison everything else you have on offer is a bit dull. It is a case of the classic break up phrase in reverse, 'it's not them, it's you!'

If you think about your environment, especially indoor, where have you created any sort of area of provision that will allow those children to explore their desire to take a risk, to get a knot in their stomach at the anticipation of possible cause and effect?

I am not suggesting that you build a bike track on your carpet area, but rather than just removing the problem it is worth trying to look beyond the bikes to what it is that the bikes provide that nothing else does.

I have found that it can be as simple as constructing towers with large cardboard boxes. Working in one setting who had the 'bike issue' we introduced a stack of large cardboard boxes for the children to build with. They were able to build them high with the very exciting addition of a step ladder. They built them quickly, because of the size of the boxes. They were dwarfed by the height of the tower. But best of all, when they had built it and engaged in all of the language and knowledge that goes along side that process, they got to knock it down!

For many children (especially boys) without the thrill then, you don't get the will and without the will there is little or no chance of engaging them in learning a new skill. So when it comes to 'difficult to engage' children in your continuous provision think three words: thrill, will and skill!

Case study Skill development

St Thomas More RC Primary school in Coventry is two form entry. Claire and her team have been having a go at introducing differentiated skills into some areas of stagnation. I visited them for a catch up at the beginning of September.

Claire and her team had clearly worked very hard over the summer because they had transformed their space. Not only was the environment clearly linked to their point of entry assessment but key areas had a weekly skill enhancement and differentiation.

This is like a huge working wall which will continually change in response to children's interests and experiences. The photographs show children engaged in activities, the speech bubbles record how the children were able to articulate their learning or interest, the cloud is a practitioner judgment and a sticky note will be added to the bottom of the cloud to show next steps. These will be transferred directly into children's learning journeys when they are taken down off the wall.

Claire has planned for skill differentiation in areas, but her headteacher (Mary) asked that this differentiation be displayed so that adults working in the setting were able to keep track. Also when Mary came in to do any monitoring (or just to play), she could easily track attainment and see how the system was working.

These are positioned way above head height so that they don't get into the children's immediate line of vision. They are there to encourage children to develop skills. They are not the same as the learning objectives that will be taught during direct teaching time.

The resources that are in the continuous provision should then reflect the skills listed. They should be 'dressed' for interest to encourage the 'target' children to use them.

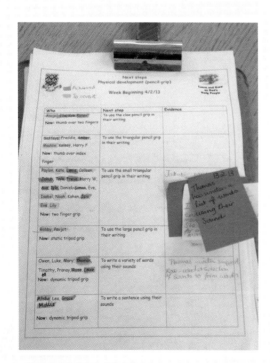

Elsewhere in Claire's continuous provision were these bobbins
that had been dressed for interest to develop the skill of
pincer grip and wrist pivot. I wonder what the children who
needed to develop this skill got excited about!

These sheets were used to develop higher level cutting skills
and again they have been dressed for interest.

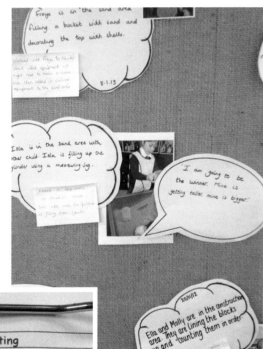

The children at St Thomas More were engaged, active and
purposeful in their learning. Activities were fun and had
been planned around the things that motivate children. The
environment was matched to assessment. The continuous
provision was also matched to assessment and further
strengthened with skill development.

The adults delivered a mixture
of direct teaching and
objective-led teaching through
continuous provision which was
producing some brilliant results
even this early in the school
year.

KEY AREA OF FOCUS	Writing
WHO AND WHAT	NEXT STEPS
Names of Children in this ability group	Uses some clearly identifiable letters to communicate meaning
Callum Daniel Bobby	
Experiments with mark making sometimes ascribing meaning to the marks.	
	Represents some

Objective-led planning and the role of the adult

Objective-led planning has to be the most effective way of taking teaching into children's play that I have ever used. With objective-led planning you would still group the children by ability based on assessment. Rather than having 'red group', 'blue group' and so on for Communication and Language, Literacy, Mathematics and so on, it allows you to group your children by their specific need in each area of learning. So, children who need more support in talk development and less in fine motor can get just that, rather than being in one ability group for both.

Once you have decided on your teaching focus you can group your children in relation to their performance within that area. For each group of children you would then make a statement of their current performance in that area to show 'where they are now' and then you plan a 'next step' for each group. It is the next step that you then take into the children's play. I would not call groups of children to me for activities, the success of objective-led planning is based on the fact that you go to them.

When you go and play alongside children you get high levels of engagement. If you come across a group of children of mixed ability, and you will, because children don't tend to play in ability groups, you just differentiate your questioning to suit the next steps objectives for the ability group of the child you are working with. If I know that I have got a group of children who have a particular interest in a particular theme such as space adventure, then I might create a 'starter activity' that I know is going to grab their interest.

Once they have visited my activity and I have fulfilled my teaching objective then I wouldn't start calling other children over. The activity has fulfilled its purpose in attracting the children that I was targeting. I would now take my objectives into other children's play.

When the children are in continuous provision, the adults will go into that play not only to look for opportunities for assessment and observation, support children's play and discovery but also to teach, delivering an objective that had been identified by assessment as a need and has then been broken down into next steps for each ability group.

This objective-led planning might be linked to the direct teaching sessions or it might be linked to any other aspect of the EYFS that your assessment and observation has identified as a need. This planning for adults in continuous provision would last for a week. During that week the adult (or adults) responsible for that objective would try to deliver it to all of the children at least once through play.

They would probably not have a planned activity that they took around the setting. Instead, they would look for opportunities to to deliver the next steps objectives through what was engaging the children most. If a child you were working with didn't understand or achieve the objective then you could revisit it a number of times in a number of different areas across the week.

By the same token if a child clearly showed that they were beyond the objective that you had set for them then you could revise that objective and deliver it to them again in a different play situation.

How do you plan for it?

For your direct teaching sessions you would differentiate your objective over 3 broad levels or more and direct your questioning to children, based on their ability level. For objective-led planning you decide on which aspect of a subject you were going to focus on. It could be calculations, talk, upper body movement, pencil grip, ability to independently access the painting area. Anything that has been identified by assessment, observation or curriculum coverage as a need.

First you group your children by their ability within this aspect.

Next, on your planning sheet, you make a statement of current attainment under each group of children. This is an important stage in the planning process because it crystallises your thoughts about what you think these children are capable of and how you know it. It also lets the whole team know what you are thinking

Then you make a 'next steps' statement of attainment for each group. This is what you are going to take with you into the play and deliver. If you go into play and you find a group of children of mixed ability, there is no need to syphon them off by their ability level, you just differentiate what you ask them guided by your 'next steps' statements on your planning sheet.

I have found that any more than 3 objectives led planning sheets in any one setting becomes hard to manage and track. In larger settings adults often double up on one ojective and just present it in different ways.

Chapter 5
Objective-led planning and
the role of the adult

Case study Dee Point Primary

Lindsay at Dee Point Primary has been trialling objective-led planning with her two form entry team.

Here is an example from the beginning of the year. The objective was centred around the children's independent use of paint and the painting area.

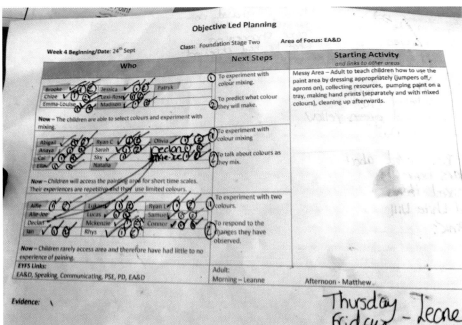

The next step for each group is split into 2 smaller steps, hence the numbering next to the children's names. The adult is going to go where they are likely to get high level engagement so the children (who all happen to be boys) who don't visit the painting area (hence their objective) are not likely to wander in any day soon.

The adult needs to engage them with the objective in a space where they like to be. Then if the adult can get them interested they might venture into the painting area.

The objective is about mixing colour and commenting on what happens. There is nothing to stop you doing this outdoors with mud and powder paint or taking your indoor provision outside for engagement and theming your outside painting station around the interests of the key group.

These planning sheets were on clipboards to make it easy for the adults to pick them up and put them down.

Where I would usually have a column for 'evidence' Lindsay has put in an example of an activity starter, just to give her team some support with this type of planning until they got their heads around it!

Any extra assessments and observations were written on the back of the sheet or on a separate sheet.

Here is an example of a different objective with assessments and observations attached:

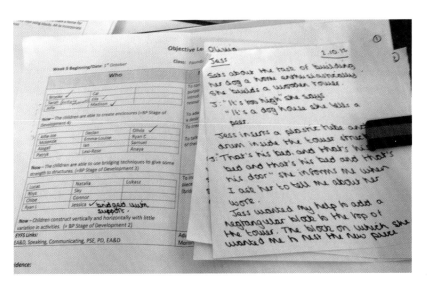

Chapter 5
Objective-led planning and
the role of the adult

Case study **Chester Blue Coat Primary**

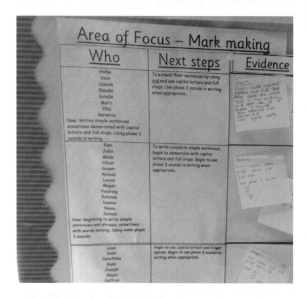

Joanne and her team at Chester Blue Coat Primary are also using this form of adult directed and then objective-led planning to great effect. They started the process in their setting by every adult having the same objective. This was done so that everyone in the team could have a shared experience of how the system works. Once everyone is comfortable with what they need to do then you would move to different adults having different objectives.

Joanne had some lovely examples of how you can translate this sort of planning and teaching into display which had been created by her and the reception team.

The one that starts with Harvey is fairly self explanatory. It also shows how one child's particular interest can spark a much bigger learning trend.

What it shouldn't do is to send us into a 'topic' planning frenzy and lead us to theme everything for half a term on magnetism!

Here is an A3 wall mounted version of objective-led planning done by Susan from St Augustine's Primary in Coventry.

The focus here was writing. Once this sheet had been completed then a member of the team would look for writing opportunities in the children's play and then encourage the children to access their 'next steps' target.

Not all of the children will be swept along in the wonderment of the magnetic world but lots will. As a result we would plan the 'next steps' objectives of what we needed to teach and then dress any that were appropriate, in magnetism for the children who were interested in magnets and for the children that weren't 'dress' theirs in something else.

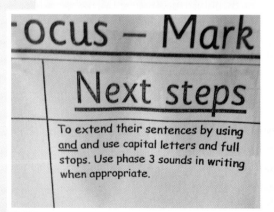

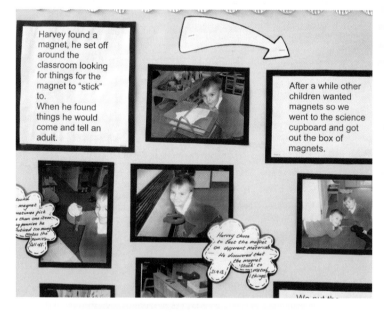

Harvey found a magnet, he set off around the classroom looking for things for the magnet to "stick" to.
When he found things he would come and tell an adult.

After a while other children wanted magnets so we went to the science cupboard and got out the box of magnets.

Next steps :- all the children will be given the opportunity to sort different objects or materials.

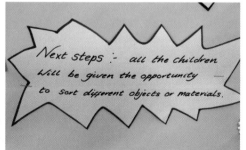

Next steps

To extend their sentences by using *and* and use capital letters and full stops. Use phase 3 sounds in writing when appropriate.

Often it is the case that our reluctant mark maker is reluctant because he doesn't see the value, or have any interest in the marks that we are asking him to make. As with everything else engagement is the key!

Elsewhere fence weaving gave some great opportunities for grip assessment as well as a high level of interest from both boys and girls.

This was then reflected in the indoor provision and differentiated for different levels of fine motor skill.

Next steps :- to continue to develop the hand and finger muscles to enable Jan to use a controlled pincer grip.

Sonny
black an
he wanted
Sonny kn.
going to
and whic
After pain
his brus.

Next Steps:
Sonny needs to access
Materials to enhance
his pictures.

and

Chapter 5
...ed planning and
...le of the adult

Maintaining an environment for learning and skill development

At several points, every day, early years settings experience a phenomenon which I call 'trash time'. No matter how well you have coached the children in the use of an area or how expertly you have labelled your resources, there comes a point where you look up from what you are doing to find that literally within the last two minutes the environment has gone from an organised learning opportunity to a scene from 'Stig of the Dump'!

This just happens because children are actively using the environment and, with the best will in the world, they are not going to always wash their paintbrushes after they have used them or put their scissors back into the right pot. When 'trash time' occurs it has a significant effect on the potential for attainment within your continuous provision.

You have used assessment to plan your areas, you have stocked them with appropriate resources. You have 'dressed' some of those resources for interest and you have even enhanced two or three areas with a skills focus. You have indeed dressed your environment for learning success. But, unless children are supported and helped to choose the right resources, unless the right scissors go back into the 'Spider Man' tin and not the princess tin, then your well laid plans are likely to fail.

One of the many benefits of objective-led planning is that the adults are mobile during continuous provision sessions. They are not stuck at one particular table or even one particular area. They are constantly moving through the space looking for opportunities to support children's learning, observe and assess them and deliver their objective. While they are on the move, the adults should also re-set any of the areas that they visit. I am not talking about a full scale tidy up, just literally a one minute re-set, either on their own or with the children. If every adult did this as a matter of course during continuous provision, not only would the environment remain more effective for teaching and learning, it would also take the children far less time to tidy up which in turn would give you more learning time.

Cha
Objective-led planning
the role of the adu

Case study Reception

How it can work

The teacher

In this reception setting there is a teacher and a teaching assistant. The teacher has a writing focus for her objective-led planning. She is going to get the children to write using their knowledge of phonics. She has grouped all of the children by their phonic knowledge and given each group a 'next steps' statement. She has not planned an activity.

The teaching assistant

The TA had got a Mathematics focus for her objective-led planning. She is working on recognition of one-digit and two-digit numbers. She wants the children to recognise, name and order numbers. She has planned a 'starter' activity. Once interest has dwindled in her activity she will leave it and take the objectives into the environment to target groups and individual children.

What we are looking at in this photo below is the TA who has whipped out a supermarket bingo set. She has not said that specific children have to come and work with her. She has used the lure of the game to get their interest and it worked. There were too many children interested to start with! The adult could have created differentiated bingo cards that would correspond to the next steps objectives that had been planned or would differentiate her questioning depending on the individual children she was working with.

Notice behind the bingo session there are two boys engaging in a bit of deconstructed role-play. They have chosen to be pirates and are hiding a small pirate chest full of gold coins in the cave (made of cardboard boxes) that they have created.

The teacher observes the boys in play and does not 'steam roller' in, clipboard in hand, but instead rolls out huge sheet of paper onto the floor. This in itself gets the interest of other children within close proximity.

She then asks the role-playing boys what is happening in their play. They are keen to tell her and she begins to draw parts of it out, creating a visual 'map' of their play. She then models labelling her drawings. All of the time she is explaining to the children who have gathered what she is doing, and then encouraging them to join in.

Many do and begin to move between the role-play and the paper, playing and then mapping their play. The teacher is supporting their learning on lots of levels but also fulfilling her writing objective differentiated to the ability level of the child she is working with.

The play takes another interesting shift when the 'map' of the role-play actually becomes the source of play with the introduction of small world characters. The play is now taking place in two places at once. A bit like a live game of Dungeons and Dragons!

The teacher ended up staying with this activity for a long time as there was lots of opportunity to meet her objectives, with a variety of children, as well as chances to support them in other areas of their learning while completing a couple of observations!

The TA on the other hand has worked with the first lot of 'bingo' children and then had enough interest to work with a second batch. Now she has moved into the environment with her objectives leaving the bingo on the table ... where it is being used by children as part of their continuous provision.

One of the many advantages of this system of planning and teaching is that if you had a child in your bingo group that wasn't able to recognise and name numbers, then you could find them later in the house and count spoons, then in the garage and count cars, then in the workshop and count pom-poms. Because you are doing it through their play you get high level engagement and they don't even know that you are doing it!

Chapter 6

Pulling it all together

If you get your continuous provision right, then you can be really secure that you are doing everything that you can to ensure that your environment has been created to continue the provision for learning in the absence of an adult.

Continuous provision by its very nature means that there is no adult in every space guiding children and promoting their learning, therefore you cannot guarantee that the children who you have aimed specific resources at in specific areas will always go to the area you want them to and put their hands on the correct resource. What you can say, is that through your planning for the provision, you have maximised the potential for attainment and minimised the risk of failure.

When you are thinking about your provision can you answer the 'why', 'who', 'how' and 'what' questions? Why is it there? Who is it there for? How will I get the target children to use the provision? What skills am I developing?

If you want to get a quick idea of whether your provision is working then do a few 'on the spot' attainment audits, tracking children who are not working with an adult and trying to equate what they do with attainment.

Another key to the success of your continuous provision is the availability of the adults in the setting to be mobile and constantly move through your space to support and develop learning. This fluidity cannot happen if every adult is tied into a space or an activity.

If you have created provision linked to assessment that is levelled and dressed for interest then all of the adults who are going to work in the space should be aware of what is where and why. This way, when they are moving through your space they will know what they are looking for and will be able to make accurate assessments as to whether the provision is being correctly accessed. If it isn't or if a child needs support or challenge they know which resources to use and how to use them.

How you plan your day and deliver your teaching is crucial in creating an appropriate environment to allow all of the above to happen. Some of your planning will be done on a daily basis in response to assessments and observations. Some can be done on a weekly basis and tweaked as and when you need to.

If you were using all of the timetabling, teaching and planning mechanisms that I have talked about in this book, on a weekly planner you would need to show your planning for:

Literacy, mathematics and phonics (or whatever your virtual base times are going to be): This planning should show differentiation and indicate which adults will be teaching which groups.

A base time planner: If you are going to teach your base time objectives through other areas of learning and through other areas of the environment then your weekly plan needs to show which adults will be in which areas of your setting for each base time. It doesn't have to say what they are teaching, just who is going where.

Talk focus for interest carpet times: This just needs to record what type of talk you will be focusing on and any key vocabulary that you would like practitioners to use. This talk will be a predominant focus at carpet times, but if adults know what the focus is then they will be able to use it throughout the setting as and when it is appropriate

Self registration continuous provision: If you are going to utilise the beginning of the day to target a specific area of learning in your continuous provision then you would need to record what that was and why you were doing it, referencing assessment data or whole school/setting initiatives.

Funky Fingers/Dough Gym activities: Depending on how many groups you have for your five minute physical intervention this could just be a simple activity list indicating any resources needed.

Objective-led planner (3 different plans delivered by 3 different adults): This is the planning that your adults will be taking with them to support teaching and learning in continuous provision. This planning needs to show which aspect you are going to be teaching, the children's current attainment in that aspect and their next steps targets. It is vital to remember that this is not a tick list and should be delivered in several areas of the environment through children's play.

Skill enhancements: If you have identified areas that you feel are stagnating and you want to enhance then with a skills focus, then your planning needs to show which areas you are focusing on, differentiation of the skill and any resourcing that you need to include to support development.

If all of the above is visible in your setting, it is not only a constant reminder for all practitioners, but it can also help anyone who is coming into your settings to judge the impact of your provision on attainment to see where you are making strong links between children's play and learning.

Versions of all of the above planning formats are available on pages 66-72.

Case study Joseph Cash Primary school

In Coventry, Nicki and the early years team at Joseph Cash Primary School have been trying their hand at levelling their continuous provision, adding skill enhancements and trialling objective-led planning.

The school has 60 reception children who work in one open plan space (with a small work room next to the toilets) and a nursery class who have their own space but share an outside area.

I was working with Nicki on the further implementation of objective-led planning and looking at their current systems for recording all of their other bits of planning – plus a bit of outdoor evaluation thrown in for good measure.

There were lots of displays that were linked to teaching and learning. They had been annotated really well so that it was clear to see engagement, planning and purpose through what was on the wall.

The work for this display was produced as a result of children working on their physical dexterity during their daily intervention. It went up the wall and across the ceiling, there was so much of it. Although the higher the display the less likely the children are to engage with it, I did come across a group of children who were lying on the floor looking up at the ceiling and picking out animal shapes that they could see in the squiggles. They were there for a while and found lots!

Some nice illustrations of process and annotations. I also really liked these as another way of creating a number line.

I imagine you would get a lot of volunteers if they knew that they were going to go and photocopy their hands! Just make sure you do it when the secretary is out of the office!

Within the provision, Nicki has been looking at levelling in response to assessment so, there were three different types of construction available not to mention the large scale construction on the carpet.

When you have planned for different levels within an area and all of the adults working in your space know what the differentiation is, when they are moving through your space it is easy for them to support children and redirect them if they are using inappropriate resources.

The reception day has two long sessions of continuous provision punctuated by focused teaching in groups and a physical intervention. The children are also grouped for this activity. On the day I visited the groups were:

- making marks on a large scale

- practising early cutting skills by snipping/fringing with appropriate scissors

- picking up pompoms with pegs (even the pegs are differentiated, some being harder to squeeze than others)

- tying tricky knots

Outside of the adult directed activities there was plenty to explore and discover in the environment, especially in the aptly name 'Hmm, this looks interesting' area where the children were deconstructing old computers and keyboards with great interest.

It was evident from the walls that observations and children's interests were key to shaping the environment and the planning.

Alongside some dough in the malleable materials area there was a nice big tray of PVA which was great for supporting gross motor movement and pattern making as well as more fine motor dexterity and mark making.

The best thing about a tray of PVA is that when your hands are covered you can clap them together and make snow. As you clap, little strands of PVA float up into the air and then come down again like stringy snow. If you bang a flat hand on the tray repeatedly you get the same effect, it is just noisier!

As part of her weekly planning process Nicki has an A4 sheet which is split into boxes, each with the title of an area of the provision. Nicki records in the box any areas that have been enhanced and says why. This was a really useful tool for me when I was looking at the provision and a great record for the setting of how they are responding to the needs and interests of children. With a relatively small 'tweak' this overview could also show which areas had a skill enhancement and how that skill was split into high, mid and low level.

Planning formats

Planning for continuous provision (Foundation Stage)

Adult	Objective	Exceeding	Expected	Expected	Emerging
Name 1	**Mathematics – Numbers** To recognise and use numerals	Recognise numerals between 10-20	Recognise numerals to 10	Recognise numerals to 5	Recognise numerals of significance Show an awareness of rhyme
Name 2	**Literacy: Writing and Reading** To demonstrate phonic awareness	Apply phonics skills when reading and writing	Attempt to represent sounds (particularly those in the initial position) correctly when writing	Identify the initial sound in a word	Identify different sounds and place them in context
Name 3	**Expressive Arts and Design** To use construction materials to build and construct	To construct with a purpose in mind	To construct and decide upon a purpose during the process of building	To construct then give a description when asked	To experiment with construction materials

Continuous Provision © Featherstone

Timetable – Foundation Stage. Who, When, Where

Adult	Day	Welcome time	Large group 1	Continuous provision AM	Continuous provision PM	Large group 2
Name 1	Mon	Read	Outside	Outside	Inside	Bay
	Tue	Read	Bay	Inside	Outside	Inside
	Wed	CP	Inside	Outside	Inside	Inside
	Thurs	Read	Outside	Inside	Outside	Outside
	Fri	CP	Large Hall	Inside	Outside	
Name 2	Mon	CP	Bay	Inside	Outside	Inside
	Tue	Read	Inside	Outside	Course	Inside
	Wed	CP	Outside	Inside	Inside	Outside
	Thurs	Read	Outside	Outside	Inside	Bay
	Fri	Read	Large Hall	Inside		
Name 3	Mon	CP	Inside	Inside	Outside	Inside
	Tue	Read	Outside	Outside	Inside	Outside
	Wed	CP	Outside	Inside	Outside	Bay
	Thurs	Read	Bay	Outside	Inside	Inside
	Fri	Read	Large Hall	Inside	Inside	
Name 4	Mon	Read	Outside	Outside	Inside	Outside
	Tue	Read	Outside	Inside	Outside	Bay
	Wed	CP	Bay	Outside	Outside	Inside
	Thurs	Read	Inside	Inside	Inside	Inside
	Fri	CP	Large Hall	Inside	Inside	
Name 5	Mon	Set outdoor equipment out		Inside	Inside	
	Tue			Outside	Float	
	Wed			Inside		
	Thurs			Outside		
	Fri			Inside		

Continuous Provision © Featherstone

Virtual Base time 1 - Foundation Stage: Week 1

Day	Monday	Tuesday	Wednesday	Thursday	Friday
Area of Learning/ Objective	**Literacy: Writing** To use letters and represent initial sounds correctly	**Mathematics: Number** To estimate then check by counting	**Literacy: Reading** To read from top to bottom, left to right and match 1:1	**Mathematics: Number** To estimate then check by counting	**Physical Development:** Moving and Handling To move freely and with pleasure in a variety of ways
Where	Outside	Bay	Inside	Outside	
Resources	Card of different sizes, pens, alphabet charts, masking tape	Blocks, sand timer	Photos of children playing with blocks with writing next to each picture	Large bucket, beanbags, drawn chalk circle, whistle	
Activity	Introduce idea that wooden blocks are going to be used as a fire engine/ fire station. Model writing first then children to label items and make badges e.g. water, hose, fire fighter, engine	Build a tower before the sand timer runs out. Count how many blocks. Repeat but this time estimate how many blocks can be built. Check by counting	Talk about what is happening in the pictures then read the captions	Play – Fill the bucket Bucket in the centre of the circle, beanbags inside the circle, when whistle blows grab a beanbag and toss into the bucket, blow whistle, estimate how many beanbags in the bucket then check by counting	

Continuous Provision © Featherstone

Virtual Base time 1 - Foundation Stage: Week 2

Day	Monday	Tuesday	Wednesday	Thursday	Friday
Area of Learning/ Objective	**Literacy: Writing** On occasion, when prompted by an adult, give meaning to marks e.g. 'that's me'	**Mathematics: Number** Apply 1:1 consistently when counting	**Literacy: Reading** Repeats words or phrases from familiar stories	**Mathematics: Number** Apply 1:1 consistently when counting	
Where	Bay	Inside	Outside	Outside	
Resources	Large white card, thick black pens	Construction pieces	Big book 'We're Going On A Bear Hunt'	Hoops	
Activity	Adult to model drawing self portrait then writing name underneath. Children to draw themselves and make marks to represent their name then give meaning to the marks	Give children an amount of construction to build with. Children to count each piece before building	Read and act out different parts with children repeating the phrases. Use different areas of the playground to represent the different environments	Play 'The Hoop Shout' Place 8 hoops on the floor. Children skip round until adult calls 'hoop' children jump in the hoop. One counter counts how many children are in each hoop	

Reflection sheet

Area: _____Creative_____   Week beginning _____

Day	What I have noticed	What I did this afternoon/tomorrow	Is there this anything that I will plan/set up?
Monday	Children using the creative resources to make their own finger puppets	Get out the mobile puppet theatre	More puppet making resources, provide real objects and books for reference and stimulus
Tuesday			
Wednesday			
Thursday			
Friday			

Continuous Provision © Featherstone

Next steps: Physical development (pencil grip)

Week beginning _____

Who	Next step	Evidence
Now: thumb over two fingers Jessica Freddie Paylon	To use the claw pencil grip in their writing	
Now: thumb over index finger Isabel Daniel Lily Eve	To use the triangular pencil grip in their writing	
Now: two finger grip Kya Katen Harry F Maddie	To use the small triangular pencil grip in their writing	
Now: static tripod grip Owen Luke Harry J	To use the large pencil grip in their writing	
Now: dynamic tripod grip Timothy Pranay Louie	To write a variety of words using their sounds	Timothy has written a list of words using their sound
Now: dynamic tripod grip Alisha Leo Grace Mollie	To write a sentence using their sounds	

Continuous Provision © Featherstone

Objective led planning

Who	Now/next
Adam Amanda Mahal Rojib	**Where they are now** Knows that a group of things changes in quantity when something is added or taken away. **Next Steps** Can find one more and one less using objects.
Iman Matthew Suzi Helen Ryan	**Where they are now** Can find one more and one less using objects. **Next Steps** Can say one more or one less of a number without counting objects.
Bethany Izzy Kian Jalen Ben	**Where they are now** Can say one more or one less of a number without counting objects. **Next Steps** Can find a total of two groups of objects by counting them altogether.

Continuous Provision © Featherstone